Original title:
Hoots and Haikus

Copyright © 2025 Creative Arts Management OÜ
All rights reserved.

Author: Matthew Whitaker
ISBN HARDBACK: 978-1-80567-189-3
ISBN PAPERBACK: 978-1-80567-488-7

Nature's Nightly Confessions

The crickets play their tunes,
With frogs joining the dance,
A raccoon steals my snacks,
In moonlit, quirky prance.

The owls whisper secrets,
In a voice soft but sly,
Stars giggle overhead,
While fireflies flash by.

The Enigma of Nightfall

Why do shadows stretch long?
A cat's leap makes no sound,
The night jester appears,
In the dark, lost but found.

The silly bats take flight,
With a flutter and swoosh,
While the moon plays peek-a-boo,
In her silver-lined hush.

Pondering Amongst the Stars

Twinkling giants above,
Winking like they know,
Is that a comet or a plane?
With each burst of glow.

I pondered and I sighed,
The cosmos spins a tale,
While aliens chuckle low,
On their interstellar trail.

Silhouettes of Memory

The trees bend with laughter,
As night whispers a jest,
I remember the odd things,
Like squirrels in a fest.

Footsteps echo softly,
A raccoon holds a grudge,
While shadows play on walls,
And giggles nudge the fudge.

Thoughts Upon the Wind

Silly whispers dance and spin,
Tickling leaves with a soft grin.
Laughter travels on a breeze,
Carrying joy among the trees.

Clouds in costumes, drifting free,
Chasing shadows, laughing glee.
The sun winks a cheeky eye,
As squirrels scamper, oh so spry.

The Palette of Dusk

Colors riot, dusk's delight,
Pastel giggles in the night.
Crickets chirp in harmony,
While stars appear, mischievously.

Glow of moon, a playful tease,
Whispers carried by the breeze.
Painting dreams on velvet skies,
Where laughter meets sleepy sighs.

Serene Shadows

In corners dark, where shadows play,
Monsters meet for light ballet.
Couch cushions turn to secret forts,
And laughter rings in funny sorts.

Whimsical shapes in twilight glow,
Bouncing nightmares, to and fro.
A giggle here, a tickle there,
As happy phantoms fill the air.

Collecting Silence

Quiet moments, a funny theft,
Stealing breezes, with no regret.
Each soft sigh, a treasure found,
A giggle caught, without a sound.

Jars of stillness, sparkling bright,
Captured whispers, pure delight.
In silence, secrets grow and swell,
In the peace, we laugh so well.

Songs of the Celestial Wanderers

Stars play tag in the dark,

Giggles that twinkle and spark.
Meteors race with pure delight,
Moonbeam dance, oh, what a sight.

Planets spin in a silly round,
Laughter echoes, a joyful sound.
Comets wink and whirl about,
In the night, they sing and shout.

Lullabies from the Timbered Realm

Whispers of trees in evening's play,

Squirrels serenade at end of day.
Branches sway, a rhythm so sweet,
Nature's band, a amusing beat.

Rubber boots tap on muddy ground,
While frogs croak out a comic sound.
Fireflies flicker in jesting flight,
Giggling shadows, a silly sight.

Mews from Above: A Nocturnal Harmony

Cats in hats on moonlit roofs,

Purring secrets, silly woofs.
Whiskers twitching, they plot and scheme,
Chasing shadows in a night dream.

Paws prance lightly, a clumsy show,
Felines laughing, stealing the glow.
Stars join in with a playful gleam,
Together, they create a theme.

The Listenings of the Moonlit Grove

Crickets chirp a playful tune,

In the company of the bright moon.
Owls chuckle from their high perch,
While fireflies wiggle in a search.

Branches rustle with cheeky flair,
While night air tickles without a care.
Laughter echoes through mossy ground,
In the grove where joy is found.

Feathered Echoes

In the moonlit night, they glide,
With a bob and a wink, they slide.
Perched on branches, eyes so wide,
Whispering secrets, with laughter tied.

Wings spread wide, they take to flight,
Making mischief, what a sight!
Chasing shadows, oh what fun,
Racing stars until it's done.

Twinkling eyes, they start to tease,
Landing softly on the breeze.
Flip a twig, and hear them glee,
Nature's jesters, wild and free.

Every chuckle breaks the calm,
Each soft call, a playful psalm.
In the dark, their antics shine,
Spreading joy, oh how divine!

Rhythm of the Owls

In the stillness, they commence,
With a bop and a little suspense.
Swooping low, then rising high,
Dance of shadows in the sky.

They hoot in sync, a jazzy tune,
Bouncing beats under the moon.
Flipping branches, catching air,
With every move, they show their flair.

Winking at the stars above,
Playing games, that's how they love.
Chaotic whispers fill the night,
As they prance in pure delight.

A feathered band with playful calls,
Echoing joy from leafy halls.
In their rhythm, let's partake,
Join the laughter, for laughter's sake!

Shadows in the Pines

Swaying softly with a chuckle,
In the pines, they make a huddle.
With playful screeches in the air,
Poised and ready, not a care.

Round and round in games of chase,
Each soft flap, a funny face.
Echoes bounce from tree to tree,
Giggles ring through canopy.

Nestled deep in dark sublime,
Whisking tunes without a rhyme.
Peeking out with eyes so bright,
Naughty whispers in the night.

With every rustle, laughter's spun,
In the shadows, oh what fun!
Dancing light beneath the stars,
These feathered friends—our secret czars!

Silent Symphony

A hush falls down, the night is ripe,
In perfect stillness, they take type.
With wings outstretched, a soft ballet,
Their silent thrums make nighttime play.

Feathers flutter like a breeze,
Quirky sounds that tease with ease.
Perching high, they plot and scheme,
In every glance, a playful dream.

Muffled hoots the stars admire,
In muted tones, they never tire.
Serenading the darkened grove,
With silent notes, their laughter rove.

Nature's jesters, evening's muse,
In soft shadows, joy's infused.
With a wink and a flapping cheer,
Their silent symphony, ever near!

Phrases Wrapped in Feathered Softness

In the quiet night air,
Chirps and giggles collide,
A feathered friend sings loud,
Tickles from the sky wide.

Bouncing on branches tall,
Jokes were whispered with glee,
Wings flapping like a ball,
Making fun of the tree.

A riddle in the dark,
Laughter echoes so bright,
Who can dance like a spark?
Only critters take flight.

Underneath the moon's grin,
Silly sounds weave a tale,
Join us in this night win,
As shenanigans sail.

Melodies of the Midnight Realm

In shadows, voices play,
Quirky tunes fill the breeze,
Squirrels join the ballet,
Swaying with utmost ease.

Owls joke about the stars,
While crickets laugh along,
A serenade from Mars,
Turns the night into a song.

As the clock strikes eleven,
Chirpy whispers abound,
They gossip 'bout the heavens,
In a chorus profound.

Feathered friends up high,
Dropping puns like confetti,
With a wink and a fly,
The night feels so ready.

The Night's Gentle Narrator

Under stars so bright,
A storyteller waits,
With each joke in sight,
Feathers dance on their plates.

A tale of lost nuts,
How the moon stole their snack,
Laughter in baby cuts,
As branches share the track.

The narrator, a hoot,
Cracks puns like a joke book,
Silly as a sweet fruit,
With a mischievous look.

In the gentle night air,
Each laugh a gentle nudge,
Stories float without care,
A lullaby to judge.

Verses in the Canopy's Breath

In the treetop's embrace,
Whispers twist and turn round,
A funny feathered race,
Where giggles can be found.

Squirrels leap and they bound,
Creating poetry quick,
With every little sound,
They write a comic flick.

A raccoon joins the fun,
Chasing tales through the leaves,
While the moon shines like sun,
Giving life to believes.

Drifting on the soft night,
Joyous verses take flight,
With each quirk, feeling right,
They dance 'til morning light.

Stolen Moments on a Branch

A squirrel steals a glance,
As birds trade silly jokes.
Perched up high and swaying,
Laughter in the oaks.

A feather lands with flair,
On a catnap-loving pup.
Dreams of flying high,
While the world wakes up.

Napping owls giggle softly,
Their wisdom, just a tease.
Chasing dreams through napping,
Life's just a breeze.

Chirps and giggles echo,
From limb to limb they roam.
Nature's stage is set,
In this cozy, leafy home.

Wisdom Wrapped in Feathers

Old owls spin tall tales,
With eyes like saucers wide.
They'd share their secrets if,
You dared to sit inside.

Squirrels crack acorn jokes,
While perched on knotted limbs.
Fuzzy cheeks and laughter,
In the dance of whims.

With every flap and flap,
They flick away the gloom.
Who knew nature could be,
A comedian's room?

Wisdom served with chuckles,
Nestled in our hair.
Next time you hear them laugh,
Join in without a care.

Midnight Monologues

The moon draws in the critters,
Stars blink at their play.
An owl clears its throat,
And the night joins the fray.

"Why did the crow caw loud?"
"Because the sky was blue!"
Each line a punchline flies,
As crickets chirp anew.

Rabbits tune their ears,
To the skits from afar.
A comedy in shadows,
Under the twinkling stars.

Wise cracks and whispers sweet,
Fill the dusky air.
As laughter echoes softly,
In the chilly lair.

Ethereal Encounters

In twilight's gentle glow,
A fox prances along.
With a cheeky grin, he sings,
A plucky, silly song.

Wings tickle the night breeze,
As owls share snickers loud.
Nature's crew is lively,
Gathered in a crowd.

The stars wink and dance,
At the antics on the ground.
With whispers of the woods,
Joy's melody is found.

Sometimes, the moonlight winks,
At the giggles down below.
In this frolicking forest,
Every laugh seems to grow.

Darkened Daydreams

A squirrel in a tie,
Dances on a fence,
Spills its nutty dreams,
Makes no sense at all.

Clouds giggle above,
While the sun plays tricks,
Jumping from behind,
Chasing shadows around.

Cats plot on the roof,
Whispering their schemes,
Flying on broomsticks,
In their wildest dreams.

A bird in a bath,
Sings to the moonlight,
With a voice so sweet,
It gives stars delight.

Eloquent Eyes of the Night

A frog in a hat,
And boots of bright green,
Croaks serenades,
To the bugs who listen.

Jellybeans rain down,
As laughter fills air,
Fireflies take flight,
Twinkling like the stars.

Mice in tiny cars,
Race 'round the barn,
Wearing shades at night,
Stealing bits of cheese.

Outside the window,
An owl hoots a tune,
To the dance of grass,
Wiggly and loose.

Perched on Silence

A parakeet dreams big,
Wearing shades and cap,
Plotting to be king,
Of a peanut land.

Crickets chirp in time,
To the rhythm of night,
While the moon laughs loud,
At their tiny show.

A hedgehog in socks,
Rolls like he's a ball,
Giggles underneath,
His prickles so proud.

Stars drop by for tea,
With sugar and cream,
Whispering secrets,
Of a dream parade.

Moonlit Musings

Bats swing and flip high,
In a wacky dance,
Chasing after light,
That glows on their wings.

A raccoon with flair,
Steals a midnight snack,
Dressed in stripes and spark,
He claims it's all art.

The night is playful,
With shadows that play,
Silly sounds echo,
In this whimsical world.

A turtle in shades,
Moves at his own pace,
Laughing at the race,
Of more hasty friends.

Twilight's Reflective Echoes

In the dusk's glow, owls wink,
With silly thoughts on the brink.
They laugh as shadows play,
Chasing the sun's last ray.

Beneath trees, whispers spin,
The crickets join in the din.
A squirrel scuttles with pride,
Mischief he cannot hide.

Branches sway with a chuckle,
As the stars begin to snuggle.
A dance of leaves in the breeze,
Nature's giggles with ease.

In this twilight, all seems merry,
As the moon keeps pace, not wary.
The night's a stage for the bold,
With secrets and tales retold.

Timeless Tales of the Forest Keepers.

Deep in woods where laughter rings,
Elders share their quirky things.
Stories of frogs who can sing,
And rabbits that wear a bling.

Mushrooms with hats in a row,
Invite the wild ones to a show.
Dancing by the moonlight's beam,
While owlets plot their ice cream dream.

Squirrels argue 'bout the best nut,
Each thinks theirs is the true cut.
While a wise old owl does stare,
With a grin, he's beyond compare.

Leaves giggle as they twirl around,
Conspiracies in whispers found.
In these woods, where joy will thrive,
Nature's playground is alive.

Whispers of the Night

In the shadows, secrets creep,
While the world prepares for sleep.
A cat with eyes of glowing jade,
Shares stories of the woodland parade.

Bats flit by in a clumsy dance,
With flip and flaps, they take their chance.
A fox sneezes—Oh what a shock!
Echoes fill the woodland block.

The moonlight shines on silly sprites,
Playing pranks throughout the nights.
They tickle twigs and tease the dew,
With giggles that are light and true.

All around, the night erupts,
With laughter as the forest clumps.
Where every shadow's got a quirk,
And no one's hushed when the fun's at work.

Secrets in the Moonlight

By the creek, where shadows blend,
A raccoon finds a fish to send.
With splashes loud, he makes a scene,
A jester fit for a moonlit keen.

Whispers echo from the pines,
As the creatures weave their lines.
A hedgehog dons a tiny crown,
Proclaiming he'll never frown.

In starlit glades, a party's near,
Where laughter rolls like a sincere cheer.
Fireflies hold their radiant lights,
To guide the way for mischievous nights.

Beneath the stars, tales entwine,
Of silly moments, so divine.
In this world where giggles bloom,
Moonlight carries every tune.

The Wisdom of Feathered Friends

A wise old owl said, "Whoo, whoo, whoo,"
When asked the secret, he just flew.
The crows all cawed, they wore a grin,
"It's not what you say, but the fun you spin!"

The parrot squawked, made quite a scene,
Telling tall tales of things unseen.
With feathers bright and laughter loud,
He won the hearts of every crowd.

Flapping about on a sunny day,
They joked and giggled, come what may.
The wisdom shared in quirky ways,
Brings laughter forth and brightens days.

So next time you're down, just glance above,
Join feathered friends, feel the love.
Their silly chats, a grand parade,
In the tree-tops, fun never fades!

Serenade of the Silent Woods

In still of night, a squirrel did bark,
While fireflies lit up the dark park.
A chorus of chirps from crickets near,
Singing loudly, nothing to fear.

The owls all hooted with glee and grace,
In their feathery suits, they found their place.
Whispers of winds carried secrets high,
While raccoons danced beneath the sky.

A nightingale fluffed her plump little chest,
Claiming her tunes were simply the best.
As night stretched on, a symphony grew,
Nature's rhythm in a lively brew.

So gather round in the quiet so good,
Heart of the forest, misunderstood.
Their melodies sparkle, a funny delight,
In the serenade of the silent night.

Twilight Chronicles of the Aviary

As the sun dipped low, birds took to the air,
A chorus of giggles floated with flair.
Canaries in gold, with beaks full of jest,
Played tag with the wind, oh, what a quest!

A blue jay teased with a smug little dance,
While finches caught bugs in their merry romance.
A parakeet jested, perched high on a line,
"Watch out, I'm diving!" And oh, what a dive!

The twilight shimmered with all their bright hues,
As owls began pondering their next cues.
The shadows looked on, amused by their play,
In the chronicles of dusk, they laughed the night away.

These tales of delight, they flap and they zoom,
No dull moments in this feathery room.
So grab your popcorn, sit tight, don't dismiss,
For twilight brings laughter you surely won't miss!

Delicate Notes on the Wind

Feathers afloat on a breeze that sways,
Songs woven gently through sunlight rays.
The finches compose a tune most absurd,
While sparrows giggle at every word.

A robin, quite proud, holds her note just right,
Chirping of breakfast at dawn's early light.
"Want worms or seeds?" she boldly asks near,
The answer? It's laughter, just loud and clear!

Wings flutter softly, a delicate dance,
With occasional mishaps, in nature's romance.
The woodpecker chuckles from the trunk of a tree,
Finding humor in everything, wild and free.

So if the wind whispers, take heed of its jest,
Join in the echoes, allow yourself rest.
For each little note is a gift from above,
A reminder that laughter is truly the love!

Nestled Thoughts Beneath Stars

In night's embrace, a grin does show,
The critters dance in moonlit glow.
A wise old owl, with winks so bright,
Tells jokes to stars that shine at night.

Beneath the canopy, shadows play,
Whispers of laughter drift away.
Squirrels join in, with acorn hats,
While fireflies flicker, like chatty bats.

A raccoon jives, quite the charmer,
His dance is bold, a furry farmer.
Even the trees sway to the beat,
They chuckle soft, on leafy feet.

As slumber calls, the giggles fade,
Under the stars, mischief is made.
Dreams take flight on feathers light,
As laughter echoes through the night.

Twilight Serenade

The sun dips low, a cheeky grin,
As twilight hums, the fun begins.
Crickets chirp their silly song,
A tune of joy, where we belong.

Bugs in bow ties, all prim and neat,
Tap dance on petals, oh what a feat!
Ladybugs laugh, their spots so bright,
They waltz through blossoms, a funny sight.

A frog in shades, croaks with flair,
Toads join in, with jigs in air.
The pond reflects, a comical view,
As nature's band plays a tune so true.

When night descends, the giggles soar,
A chorus of chuckles, forevermore.
In twilight's glow, we'll laugh and sing,
As stars come out, and joy takes wing.

Echoing Wisdom

In the forest deep, wisdom roams,
An ancient owl, with feathered homes.
He hoots advice, in riddles nice,
Yet squirrels giggle, oh what a price!

A fox with flair, brings tales to share,
Of shoes made from leaves, and no winter care.
With every twist, his stories grow,
Turning the wise into quips aglow.

The wise old tortoise, slow and grand,
Shares secret paths of the misty land.
But watch that hare, with leaps so vast,
His tales are wild, and never last.

As echoes bounce from tree to tree,
Laughter lingers, wild and free.
In every whisper, a dose of fun,
As wisdom dances, for everyone.

Nature's Lullaby

Under the moon, the cool breeze blows,
Nature hums sweet, where laughter grows.
With crickets chirping their nightly tune,
And owls gossiping, a jovial swoon.

The rustling leaves join in the fun,
As fireflies flicker, one by one.
A mouse in pajamas, snug and tight,
Dreams of cheese, through the peaceful night.

The brook babbles jokes, so light and clear,
While badger stands by, giving a cheer.
Turtles chuckle, as they swim slow,
In this laughter-filled ebb and flow.

As sleep descends, the giggles remain,
Nature's lullaby, a joyful refrain.
With stars as pillows, dreams take flight,
In a world of laughter, oh what delight!

Nature's Hidden Lyrics

In the woods, a crow caws,
As squirrels plot their grand heist.
Leaves rustle, secrets shared,
Nature's fun, a little sliced.

A frog leaps, so full of pride,
Splashing water, what a sight!
Caterpillars dance with glee,
In their paper-thin flight.

Bumblebees buzz, quite the crooners,
Singing to flowers, bright and loud.
Even the ants, tiny tune-makers,
March to music, head held proud.

Sunset whispers, chuckles near,
As nightfall blankets the grass.
Fireflies twinkle like silly stars,
The world laughs as shadows pass.

Cinematic Whispers

In the park, a dog runs fast,
Chasing shadows, paws a-flash.
A duck quacks, it's quite the scene,
Waddling hero, with a splash.

Under the bench, a cat snores,
Dreaming of tuna, what a prize!
Nearby, kids giggle and squeal,
Eating ice cream, sticky pies.

A squirrel stars in its own reel,
As it prances, cheeky grin.
With each jump, it takes the cake,
In this film, it's set to win.

Cinema of the everyday,
Where laughter blooms in every frame.
Nature's antics, no retakes here,
Even the grass plays the game.

Murmurings from Afar

Whispers float on the cooling breeze,
Dandelions tell a tale.
A ladybug races a butterfly,
Both gliding on nature's trail.

Crickets strum their nightly song,
While owls hoot out their quips.
The moon winks down, a bright spot,
As stars join in, with little flips.

Gophers peek, then dart away,
Nervous jokes in the tall grass.
Raccoons rummage for snacks well earned,
Their heist, a comedic class.

Echoes of laughter fill the air,
As twig-folks frolic and play.
The world, a stage, where mirth unfolds,
With nature's script, come what may.

Embraced by Darkness

Owls on the prowl,
Wings whisper soft sighs,
Mice play hide and seek,
Under moonlit skies.

Sneaky shadows dance,
As critters take flight,
Laughter echoes loud,
In the heart of night.

Branches creak and sway,
As ghosts tell their tales,
While night critters scheme,
And humor prevails.

In this cozy gloom,
Nutty antics thrive,
Even bats can smile,
When they feel alive.

Twilight Tributes

Stars begin to blink,
As the day bows down,
Crickets tune their strings,
In the grassy town.

Fireflies go winking,
With their tiny lights,
A sparkly parade,
Joy takes little flights.

Moonbeams share a laugh,
With the timid night,
Silly shadows play,
Under silver light.

Every leaf's a muse,
Telling jokes on trees,
Nature shares a grin,
With a rustling breeze.

In the Company of Night

Midnight snacks await,
In the cupboard's lair,
Squirrels act like kings,
While everyone's bare.

A dance of the owls,
With a jig and a twirl,
Their hoots are like jokes,
In a dizzy swirl.

Badgers with sly looks,
Plot mischief with flair,
While bad puns are spun,
In the cool night air.

Batty buddies buzz,
Around trees they zoom,
While the globe spins 'round,
In the darkened room.

Celestial Chronicles

The cosmos is bright,
With giggles and grins,
Stars tickle the night,
Where the fun begins.

Comets cut a path,
With a wink and a slide,
While planets, they laugh,
In this cosmic ride.

Galaxies spin tales,
Of cosmic delight,
As starlight unveils,
The dance of the night.

Nebulas compose,
Songs of joy and cheer,
In a universe wild,
Bringing laughter near.

Shadows of the Woodland Choir

In the trees, the shadows dance,
Little critters take a chance.
Singing songs of night and fun,
While the moon becomes their sun.

A squirrel shakes its tiny tail,
Echoes of a whispered gale.
Laughter floats on midnight air,
Nature's jesters everywhere.

Raccoons waddle, plotting schemes,
Dreaming up their wacky themes.
Bats chime in with silly flaps,
Performing for the woodland chaps.

Amidst the laughs, a silly show,
In the dark, their antics glow.
Together, they create delight,
In the shadows of the night.

An Ode to the Nocturnal Whisperers

Whooo cooks up the midnight feast?
Is it mouse, or cat, or beast?
Owl eyes wide with mischief bright,
Plotting antics for the night.

Under stars, the whispers float,
A raccoon wears a funny coat.
He prances round without a care,
While shadows twist in cheerful flair.

Hedgehogs wear the finest spines,
Critters gather for the lines.
Silly chatter fills the air,
Echoes make a lovely pair.

As laughter bubbles, echoes tease,
The nighttime chorus sings with ease.
Each giggle shared beneath the moon,
Turns the quiet night to tune.

Rhymes Beneath the Stars

Beneath the twinkling starlit dome,
Creatures gather far from home.
In the fields, the laughter blooms,
Echoes dance through leafy rooms.

Fireflies flash like tiny lights,
Critters join in silly flights.
A badger dons a snazzy hat,
As the wise old owl chirps, "What's that?"

Squirrels spin from branch to branch,
Leaping through the woodland dance.
Each toppled leaf becomes a joke,
As nature's laughter gently woke.

In this harmony of cheer,
Even shadows have their sphere.
Underneath the vast expanse,
Creatures waltz in starry dance.

Flight Patterns in Verse

Little wings in evening skies,
Sketch the tales of owls that fly.
With a twist and turn, they say,
"Watch us whirl, we're on display!"

Bats zoom by with squeaks and spins,
Making jokes as nighttime begins.
In the dark, they tease the light,
Chasing stars with all their might.

A flutter here, a swoop and glide,
Nature's laughter, side by side.
Each swoosh of air, a jolly cue,
For feathered friends to laugh anew.

With each dive, a comic twist,
In the dark, no joy's amiss.
Nighttime dance, a gleeful chase,
In the sky, they find their place.

Whispered Words in the Wilderness

In the woods where creatures dance,
A squirrel plots with cheeky glance.
He gathers acorns for a feast,
Inviting friends, a furry beast.

The owl sings its nightly tune,
While raccoons party under moon.
Together they toast with starry eyes,
Planning mischief, oh what a surprise!

A deer reads jokes from a tree,
Laughs echo through the canopy.
With every giggle, the leaves do sway,
Nature's comedy on display.

Laughter ripples like water's flow,
As critters chuckle, 'Oh, what a show!'
In the wilderness, where fun takes flight,
Whispered words make the night feel bright.

Enchanted Observations

In the garden, fairies play,
With tiny hats and flowers gay.
They giggle, twist, and fly about,
Sprinkling joy, there's never doubt.

A grumpy frog sits on a log,
Complaining loud, oh what a slog!
But the butterflies just tease away,
Dancing 'round him, come what may.

A hedgehog juggles berries red,
While the chipmunk cheers, "Accurate!"
The sunbeams laugh, shine down aglow,
As nature's circus steals the show.

Underneath the twinkling stars,
The night unfolds, no need for cars.
With every glance, there's something new,
Enchanted tales to amuse the crew.

Sonorous Shadows

In moonlit woods, the shadows prance,
A waltz of whispers, what a chance!
The owls hoot in sync, oh dear,
As shadows giggle, swaying near.

The rabbits play a game of chase,
While fireflies light their secret space.
With every leap, they tumble down,
A furry troupe, king and clown.

Beneath the trees, the night unfolds,
With secrets shared, as laughter molds.
A squirrel dances, flips and twirls,
Nature's rhythm fills the swirls.

In the dark, a joke is told,
A secret whispered, purest gold.
Through sonorous shadows, joy we find,
In every corner, humor's kind.

The Calm of the Canopy

High above, where branches sway,
A sloth yawns in a lazy way.
He stretches limbs, then drifts to dreams,
While below, the laughter beams.

The toucan sports a beak so bold,
Telling tales that never grow old.
With colors bright and silly sounds,
The canopy's joy absolutely abounds.

Monkeys swing with playful glee,
Flipping and flopping, wild and free.
They share tales of their wild quest,
In the calm, they smile, feeling blessed.

As sunlight dapples through the leaves,
Nature chuckles, oh what it weaves!
In the calm of the canopy's shade,
Funny moments, never fade.

Echoes of the Night Sky

In the stillness up high,
An owl does a silly dance,
Flapping its wings like crazy,
Chasing shadows in a trance.

Stars wink and giggle softly,
While the night sings a tune,
A chorus of chirps and hoots,
Underneath the round moon.

Laughter of crickets echoes,
As they play a game of tag,
Lighting bugs join the fun,
As darkness starts to brag.

The sky is a canvas bright,
With dreams that twist and twine,
Each creature joins the jest,
In the still and starry shine.

Whispered Wings at Dusk

As twilight gently settles,
Wings flutter and take flight,
Birds tell their stories loud,
Bringing laughter to the night.

One by one, they swoop low,
In a wacky little race,
With a twist and turn so wild,
Each flap a funny face.

The trees are all a-titter,
As branches sway and swing,
Rippling with the breeze's breath,
Riddles the night will bring.

A playful spirit dances,
Amongst the dusky boughs,
Nature's funny caricature,
Earning laughter and applause.

Luminous Eyes Amongst the Pines

In the shades of ancient woods,
Beady eyes start to gleam,
They peek out with mischief,
Like characters from a dream.

With a hoot or a snicker,
They hide behind thick bark,
Daring one another to come,
To play in the dark.

A squirrel shares tales of jump,
While raccoons roll with glee,
Their giggles echo softly,
Among the swaying trees.

Every glimmer, every blink,
Holds a secret fun-filled plan,
An adventure through the night,
With a wild, woodsy clan.

Secrets in the Moonlight

Underneath the silver glow,
Whispers float on the breeze,
Creatures planning silly schemes,
Among the rustling leaves.

A fox dons a crafty grin,
As it sneaks through the grass,
While a badger laughs aloud,
Trying not to let time pass.

The trees shake with laughter,
As owls swap funny tales,
Drawing maps of moonlit quests,
And riding on the gales.

The night wears a gown of joy,
With secrets tucked away,
Each moment wrapped in humor,
In the moonlight's playful sway.

Nighttime Narratives

Under the moon's bright grin,
Squirrels dance in a spin,
Owls share tales of flight,
While shadows leap in delight.

Glow worms flash a bright show,
Frogs croak tunes from below,
A raccoon juggles some fruit,
While a cat plays the flute.

Stars wink down from their place,
As crickets join the chase,
A hedgehog rolls in the grass,
Laughing as moments pass.

Midnight snacks, what a treat,
Everyone wants some sweet,
While the world softly snores,
The night fun never bores.

Softly Spoken Sonnets

Whispers in a breezy tone,
A ghost cat searching for its bone,
Stars giggle, twinkling bright,
As puppies bark with pure delight.

A hedgehog wears a tiny hat,
Waddling 'round like a fancy brat,
Fireflies twirl, a sparkling dance,
Making critters giggle in a trance.

Wishes carried on the breeze,
A sleepy owl scratches with ease,
Moonbeams tickle the pond so clear,
Mirroring laughter we all can hear.

Join the fun, the night is young,
With every song that's ever sung,
In this world of giggles, truth,
Even shadows share their youth.

Whisked Away by the Wind

Kites swirl high with silly strings,
Chasing clouds on zephyr's wings,
A squirrel slips on acorn hats,
While rabbits play hopscotch with bats.

Dandelions dance, so carefree,
As if held up by a jolly spree,
Frogs leap over giggling streams,
While the sun bounds in childhood dreams.

Leaves join in with their rustling cheer,
A butterfly twirls, without any fear,
The breeze carries all silly things,
As laughter from the garden springs.

In this joyful, dizzy play,
Nature teases on her way,
With every gust, a chuckle's made,
Creating mischief in the glade.

Luminescent Lines

Scribbling dreams in light of night,
Words take flight, a pure delight,
Pixies giggle at the fun,
As paper boats drift on the run.

Moonlit paths twirl and weave,
Stories bloom, never leave,
Bouncing thoughts like springing frogs,
As laughter dances with the smogs.

Candles flicker, shadows play,
Each line a game, in a quirky way,
Mistakes become the best of cheers,
Erasers vanish in the jeers.

Join this chase of playful minds,
Where joy in every word finds,
In the glow of the simple light,
The night bursts forth, a pure delight.

Starlit Soliloquy

Beneath the moon's wide grin,
The owls hold court, begin.
With eyes like shiny marbles,
They plot and laugh at garbles.

A squirrel, quite a show-off,
Takes a leap, with a scoff.
The shadows dance with glee,
In nightly revelry.

Wings flap in the cool air,
As rabbits join the fair.
Tickles of grass and twirls,
Nature's jests unfurl.

A sudden hoot, a leap,
Comedic dreams so deep.
In laughter's soft embrace,
The stars join in the chase.

Echoes of Dusk

The sun dips down to play,
While crickets start their sway.
A frog croaks like a king,
Beneath the twilight's wing.

The wind starts to giggle,
As leaves begin to wiggle.
A mischief-maker's tune,
With laughter 'neath the moon.

Fireflies blink in jest,
In nature's lively fest.
They shuffle to and fro,
With secret tales to show.

As shadows twist and twine,
Each creature starts to shine.
In night's playful embrace,
They join the wild race.

Secrets on the Breeze

Whispers float through the trees,
Carried soft by the breeze.
A cat with a sly wink,
Plans mischief at the sink.

A raccoon wears a mask,
At night, he loves to bask.
He rummages for snacks,
And grins behind the cracks.

The owls have tales to trade,
From shadows long displayed.
Their laughter fills the night,
In a comical flight.

As stars begin to blink,
The night lends space to think.
With each secret that drifts,
The humor gently lifts.

Mysterious Murmurs

In the hush of the night,
Sounds creep close with delight.
A raccoon lifts a snack,
On a stealthy little track.

The moon rides high and bright,
As critters take their flight.
With giggles in the dark,
And whispers like a spark.

The owls congregate wise,
With laughter in disguise.
Their secrets softly weave,
In a tale hard to believe.

A rustling in the brush,
Brings a comedic hush.
As night reveals its jest,
All nature is blessed.

Reflections from the Trees

In the branches, whispers play,
Squirrel debates with a jay.
Nuts in pockets, all the rage,
Each tree's a little stage.

Leaves chuckle with a breeze,
Tales of owls and busy bees.
Sunshine tickles bark and stem,
Nature's giggles, just a gem.

Raccoon faces, masks of fun,
Sneaking tricks 'til day is done.
On the ground, the shadows dance,
Life's a wild, wacky prance.

Sap-sipping birds in a choir,
Creating tunes that never tire.
Nature's comedy held up high,
For all the critters passing by.

Stories in the Stillness

Silence holds a jestful grin,
As crickets start their nightly din.
The moon grins wide, stars come alive,
While fireflies do their little jive.

Sitting still, a frog leaps light,
Landing near—oh what a sight!
Tales are spun without a sound,
Echoes dance around the ground.

A shadowed fox begins to stalk,
Practicing its sneaky walk.
But with a hop, a bushy tail,
It slips away, without a trail.

Among the quiet trees, they weave,
Stories only they believe.
Night unveils its playful art,
Laughter beats within the heart.

Curious Calls in the Night

Whooo called out from the dark,
An owl took off with a spark.
The night was ripe with funny sounds,
As mischief in the air abounds.

A raccoon's giggle, soft and sly,
Echoes 'neath the starry sky.
The frogs join in, a chorus bright,
A symphony of pure delight.

What was that? A rustling leaf!
A sneaky hound? Or just a thief?
The night is full of silly tones,
With laughter in its hidden groans.

Crickets chirp a comic play,
Each note a joke along the way.
As night unfolds its joyful plight,
The world is fun in the moonlight.

Flickers of Folklore

Beneath the trees, stories gleam,
Like fireflies in a twilight dream.
Tales of trolls and dancing sprites,
Whispered softly through the nights.

Napping gnomes by the mossy rocks,
Tickled by butterflies and socks.
Laughter spills from ancient roots,
As fairies play their silly flutes.

A wandering shadow, what could it be?
Perhaps a spider with a tea party spree?
Or an elf who's lost his hat,
Searching now for where it's at.

These flickers glow with joyous cheer,
Woven tales for all to hear.
In the forest's playful dance,
Each breeze offers a comic chance.

Sylvan Secrets

In the woods where shadows laugh,
Trees gossip on the path,
Squirrels waltz with acorn hats,
Chipmunks play on cunning mats.

Mossy stones hold secret tales,
Frogs croak songs with vibrant wails,
A raccoon hums a silly tune,
While fireflies dance to the moon.

Branches sway with silly glee,
Whispering jokes to the bee,
Breezes tease the leaves with flair,
Nature's jesters everywhere.

So come join this merry crew,
In the wild where laughter grew,
Every twist and turn, oh boy,
The forest holds a world of joy.

Whispers of the Woodlands

In bark-clad homes where critters dwell,
A wise old owl spins tales to tell,
Bunnies giggle in the grass,
As time, it seems, does quickly pass.

Foxes play tag in the dusk light,
Chasing shadows, what a sight,
With every laugh, the stars appear,
A symphony of woodland cheer.

Hares with hats of leafy green,
Jump and jig like they're on screen,
Rustling leaves with funny sounds,
As joy and laughter there abounds.

The forest floor is their parade,
With every step, new games are played,
In this realm, so full of mirth,
Nature's fun is endless worth.

Rhythms of Reflection

A pond ripples with a splash,
Frogs engage in leap and crash,
Reflections dance with silly grace,
Every ripple wears a face.

Tall grasses bend, they sway along,
Joining in the water's song,
A shadow fights to catch its form,
In playful moves, it will transform.

Beetles break into a race,
Bouncing round with merry pace,
Each petal floats, a giggle bright,
As butterflies take joyful flight.

Who knew silence could be loud?
With nature's quirks, we feel so proud,
In every splash and rustling sound,
A laughing world is always found.

Night's Embrace

As night descends with twinkling eyes,
Creatures stir under starry skies,
An owl calls with a cheeky hoot,
While bats throw night-time dances in a suit.

Fireflies blink, a dim parade,
Lighting paths where secrets wade,
A hedgehog scurries, off to play,
In midnight escapades, they sway.

Crickets chirp their little songs,
As starlight wraps where laughter belongs,
Every shadow wears a grin,
Under the moon's gentle spin.

The night is full of whispered cheer,
With every giggle bringing near,
So join the fun, don't hesitate,
In nocturnal joy, celebrate!

The Ballad of the Silent Flight

In dim-lit woods, a whisper drifts,
A bouncing ball, the owl's misfits.
With wings so wide, they glide and weave,
A dance of night, with tricks up their sleeves.

They hoot in jest, yet blink with glee,
As rabbits laugh, "Is that you or me?"
A serenade for the moon so bright,
To join their fun on this silly night.

With eyes like saucers, they soar so high,
Chasing their shadows, oh me, oh my!
Each flap a jest, a flap like a wink,
A giggle in the air, make you think!

At dawn they gather, tired yet spry,
"Let's not go home, let's just fly high!"
The dawn, the laughter, from trees they fall,
These jokester owls, they enchant us all.

Enchanted by the Nightingale's Call

Under the stars, a chirp so sweet,
A nightingale calls, can't stay in your seat.
The owls perk up, with a quake and sway,
"Is that a tune, or just a buffet?"

"Don't look so serious, lend me your ear,
This song's for the brave, not for the deer!"
With flutters of laughter, they glide through the mist,
As crickets compose tunes, none can resist.

A shiver of giggles, the woods come alive,
With every soft note, the shadows contrive.
"Owls do the jig, let's dance till the morn,
We'll twirl 'round the trees 'til first light is born!"

And so they sang, till the dawn broke free,
With feathers a-shimmer in joyous decree.
In this twilight frolic, the nightingale grins,
As owls and their silliness whirl 'round like spins.

Owlsong: Notes from the Twilight

In twilight's hush, a chorus begins,
The owls spin tales, with mischievous grins.
They croon about whispers, with whispers of light,
As shadows dance lightly, lost in the night.

"Oh look at that squirrel," one owl might say,
"Wearing a hat, what a curious display!"
A raucous of laughter, a high-pitched squawk,
While trees sway gently, it's quite the talk.

With a hoot of mirth, they join the parade,
In feathered delight, their antics displayed.
A history of jest, where secrets are spun,
With every bold lyric, they rise, they run.

So come all you dreamers, and join in the fun,
For twilight's a stage, where mischief is spun.
In the heart of the woods, let's shout and spread cheer,
With every note sung, we'll banish all fear!

Echoes of the Woodland Lyric

Beneath the tall trees, where whispers begin,
The owls hold court, with laughter and sin.
They chuckle and sway, in verses so bright,
As echoes of joy make the shadows take flight.

"Who left the acorn?" one wise owl calls,
"Not me!" shouts another, as nighttime enthralls.
With winks and with nods, they share in the jest,
For what's better than laughter? They're feeling so blessed.

In croaks and in hoots, a symphony plays,
Of woodland revels through magical days.
With feathers a-fluffing, they dance in delight,
Making memories dance in the glow of moonlight.

With stories spun sweetly, they linger awhile,
As echoes of laughter resound with a smile.
In a woodland reverie, dreams take their flight,
Where owls weave their tales in the soft silver night.

Soft Shadows and Sweet Serenades

In the garden, shadows play,
A cat chirps at the fading day.
The moonlight dances on the lawn,
As critters giggle and dawns are drawn.

A socks-stealing raccoon prances,
While owls watch with sideways glances.
A chorus of frogs begins to croak,
In this twilight where laughter's woke.

Stories Carried on Feathered Wings

Birds in hats, oh what a sight,
They gossip and chatter, taking flight.
Each tale spun in chirps and tweets,
Of lost breadcrumbs and wormy treats.

A penguin on roller skates,
Skids and spins while joy awaits.
With wings outstretched, they make their way,
To spread the joy of a sunny day.

Whispers of the Quiet Guardian

An owl in glasses reads the news,
While raccoons debate their favorite shoes.
They chuckle softly, planning schemes,
In this woodland where laughter gleams.

A gentle fox dons a bow tie bright,
Reciting puns that spread delight.
In the stillness, giggles swell,
As night unfolds its funny spell.

Nightfall's Gentle Reverie

Stars twinkle like mischief's wink,
As critters gather, all in sync.
A mouse sings low, a wise old tune,
Under the gaze of a winking moon.

Bats fashion capes, oh what a view,
While fireflies flash with humor too.
In this night of silly dreams,
The forest glows with laughter's beams.

Feathers and Fantasies

In a tree an owl sat,
Wearing spectacles, oh so fat!
He hooted for the moon's delight,
Reciting poems all through the night.

The squirrels laughed, they danced around,
In silly antics, joy was found.
With acorns flying left and right,
Chasing dreams 'neath silver light.

Fanciful tales spun from his beak,
Of flying fish and cows that speak.
While the stars rolled their twinkling eyes,
At the antics of their feathered wise.

The night was bright, the fun was grand,
As trees became a wonderland.
With laughter echoing through the sky,
As dreams took flight, oh my, oh my!

Sweet Symphony of the Starlit

Underneath the stars so bright,
Frogs sang tunes of pure delight.
Crickets chimed their tiny song,
In harmony, they sang along.

A firefly lit the stage so clear,
Tiny dancers drew quite near.
With tiny toadstools as their ground,
They twirled and hopped without a sound.

The owls couldn't help but stare,
Wondering how without a care.
These merry creatures took to flight,
In a whimsical waltz, oh what a sight!

Morning dew began to peek,
As sleepy heads were heard to speak.
The symphony came to an end,
With waves and dreams that gently blend.

Looming Legends

Once a lion thought he'd roar,
But tripped over a tasty core.
He tumbled down into the briar,
And giggled at his sudden fire.

An owl perched on a crooked tree,
Said, 'Roar or not, just let it be!'
Together they shared a laugh or two,
While sipping tea from leaves so blue.

The world outside turned wild and bright,
As legends grew in the warm twilight.
With tales of beasts and creatures all,
Their giggles echoed, a merry call.

Soon the night turned to morning light,
With stories woven, oh what a sight!
From lions who learned to dance and prance,
To owls who loved a jolly chance.

Nurtured by Night

In the shade where shadows play,
A raccoon sneaked to steal away.
With cookies balanced on each paw,
He chuckled at the silly law.

A fox joined in with crafty glee,
Waggling tails by the old pine tree.
They planned a feast for two that night,
Chasing dreams till morning's light.

They pranked the bats that flitted by,
Those mischievous pals who flew so high.
With giggles echoing through the trees,
They danced together in the breeze.

As dawn approached, they shared a grin,
With crooked hats made from a tin.
Nurtured by laughter under starlit skies,
Their friendship grew where joy never dies.

Verses in the Twilight

In twilight's glow, they gather near,
With eyes so bright, they show no fear.
A bobble here, a wobble there,
They hoot and laugh, no time to spare.

They lead the dance among the leaves,
With silly steps, the forest heaves.
Chirping jokes, they take their flight,
What a sight in fading light!

With every flap, they crack a grin,
In this crazy world, let the fun begin!
A twist of fate in the night's embrace,
Their giggles echo, a wild chase.

So bring your friends, don't be late,
Join quirky tales, and celebrate.
In twilight's arms, the laughter swells,
Where hilarious stories cast their spells.

Wings of the Night

When night falls softly, mischief looms,
Feathers ruffled, dispelling glooms.
A flick of wings, a silly sound,
Laughter lifts, spinning all around.

They take to skies in awkward flight,
With flappy moves, they claim the night.
Belly laughs in the moonlit air,
Our feathery friends with flair to spare!

Around the trees, they make a scene,
Joking all, where none have been.
What's that over there? A bush that shakes!
A sneaky prank, for laughter's sake.

Under starry skies, they flit and glide,
In every jest, pure joy allied.
So at night's whim, let silliness bloom,
With wings of glee, in the shadows loom.

Gentle Rhymes of the Forest

In gentle woods, the echoes play,
With silly quirks in a breezy sway.
Branches shimmy, leaves say "Hi!",
While critters tell tales that make us cry.

A wise old owl, perched with glee,
Shares tired puns but you'll agree.
With every rhyme, a chuckle bursts,
Creating joy, quenching our thirsts.

A bushy tail flicks, a creature peeks,
Storytellers in playful streaks.
The moon's wide grin lights up the fun,
Each verse a giggle, never done.

Through tangled roots, a chorus sings,
Jokes and laughs on feathered wings.
In forest tales, we become entwined,
Where humor and nature are sweetly aligned.

Owlish Reflections

Upon a branch, they sit and jest,
With knowing looks, they seem the best.
Wise yet wacky, in twilight's shade,
Their quirky antics dance and fade.

With eyes so round, they start to tease,
Silly tales waft through the breeze.
"Did you hear?" one whispers low,
"Why chickens fly, we may not know!"

With chuckles soft, they share a plot,
Every giggle twinkles, hitting the spot.
Reflecting joy in a moonlit swirl,
Turned upside down, their worries unfurl.

So gather 'round, without a care,
In owlish wisdom, absurdities flare.
With laughter echoing through the night,
In all their wit, they take delight.

www.ingramcontent.com/pod-product-compliance
Lightning Source LLC
Chambersburg PA
CBHW051629160426
43209CB00004B/580